Migration to Australia

Migration From Europe

William Day

First published 2017 by
Redback Publishing
PO Box 357 Frenchs Forest NSW 2086
Australia

978-1-925630-08-4

Author: William Day
Editor: Margie Tubbs
Designer: Redback Publishing

Original illustrations © Redback Publishing 2017
Originated by Redback Publishing

Printed and bound in China by Leo Paper

Acknowledgements
Abbreviations: l—left, r—right, b—bottom, t—top, c—centre, m—middle
We would like to thank the following for permission to reproduce photographs: (Images © shutterstock) Fromt cover t Ververidis Vasilis, Front cover b Janossy Gergely, p8 TK Kurikawa, p9 ChameleonsEye, p13t TK Kurikawa, p15b Kiev.Victor, p17 rook76, p17b amophoto_au, p20 Leonard Zhukovsky, p21t Keystone Pictures USA / Alamy Stock Photo, P21m neftali, p25 FOR ALAN / Alamy Stock Photo, p26 MarKord, p27 Boris15, p29 df028, p30 Alizada Studios, p31 Northfoto

Every effort has been made to contact copyright holders of any material reproduced in this book. Any omissions will be rectified in subsequent printings if notice is given to the publisher.

National Library of Australia Cataloguing-in-Publication entry

Creator: Day, William, author.
Title: Migration from Europe / William Day.
ISBN: 9781925630084 (hardback)
Series: Migration to Australia.
Target Audience: For primary school age.
Subjects: Immigrants--Australia.
Australia--Emigration and immigration--Juvenile literature.
Europe--Emigration and immigration--Juvenile literature.

Contents

Reasons for Migration to Australia

Work

People have been arriving to work in Australia since pre-colonial times. Australia has needed migrants to provide the skills and labour for development since it was founded in 1788.

Family

Joining family members who have already migrated to Australia has been a strong pull factor in encouraging people to leave their country of birth.

Asylum

Wars and conflict around the world have caused thousands of people to seek asylum outside their own countries.

Religion

Freedom of religion is enshrined in the Australian Constitution. People who have suffered discrimination because of their religion have found that they can practise their religion freely in Australia.

Freedom

Australia is a stable democracy with freedom of speech, freedom to travel, equality for all and access to an independent legal system.

Home Ownership

Australia has a land ownership system that gives people assured title to property they have purchased. This is not the case in all countries.

Business

Australia provides educated workers and the infrastructure needed to set up successful businesses.

Education

Australian universities and colleges rank well compared with other countries. A degree from an Australian university is recognised in most countries around the world.

Health Care

Australian citizens and residents with appropriate visas have access to a health care system which provides free hospital care and treatment by a doctor who bulk-bills at no charge to the patient.

Lifestyle

Australia offers migrants a predominantly safe and friendly environment. Its beautiful landscapes and variety of climates, from tropical to alpine, attract both tourists and people wanting to settle permanently.

Top 10 Countries of Birth in Australia (2015)

Country of birth	Number of migrants	% of the Australian population
United Kingdom	1,207,000	5.1%
New Zealand	611,400	2.6%
China	481,800	2.0%
India	432,700	1.8%
Philippines	236,400	1.0%
Vietnam	230,200	1.0%
Italy	198,200	0.8%
South Africa	178,700	0.8%
Malaysia	156,500	0.7%
Germany	125,900	0.5%

In 2016, 28% of Australia's population were born overseas.

World Cultures

World cultures are divided by using terms that include:

> Western, Eastern, Middle Eastern, Near Eastern, Asian, Polynesian

These adjectives refer to a lifestyle rather than a strictly-defined geographical region. At different times throughout history, some countries have been described by one or more of these terms.

Australia is called a 'western' country because of the way people live and the style of government, even though it is nowhere near western Europe.

World Geography

Countries of the world are grouped into geographic regions. The main ones are:

> Europe, Middle East, Asia, Southeast Asia, Pacific, Oceania, the Americas, North America, Africa

Political and religious events have resulted in some countries being classed in different regions throughout their history. For example, some people place Pakistan in the Middle East, while others locate it in Asia.

How the United States Affected Immigration to Australia

Political events in the United States led to an increase in the number of people coming to Australia during two periods separated by 150 years.

Convicts

Before Australia was founded, Britain had been sending its convicts to the American colonies. After the American War of Independence, Britain had to find somewhere else to send its convicts. The settlement at Sydney Cove in 1788 was a direct result of this need to empty Britain's overcrowded prisons.

The Immigration Act of 1924

In 1924, the United States passed the Immigration Act. This act restricted the number of people they would take as migrants each year from any one country. Migrants who missed out on entering the United States had to find another destination. Australia was one of the choices available to them.

White Australia Policy

From 1901 to 1973, immigration to Australia was restricted by the White Australia Policy. The Australian government wanted to maintain Australia as an outpost of Great Britain, with a British culture and a population which was mostly British. Multiculturalism was not acceptable, and migrants from Europe were expected to assimilate, so that the British traditions that most Australians treasured would not be lost.

Migrants from Asia and other non-European places were thought to be too different in appearance and culture to ever be able to assimilate and make a contribution to the nation. In addition, Australian workers feared losing their jobs to people who might accept lower wages.

With increases in world travel, and the role of television and other mass media in increasing public awareness, Australia recognised that migrants from many countries would be able to settle harmoniously in Australia and contribute to its economy.

New Australia Colony

Although the history of Australian migration has largely been about the people who left other countries and came to Australia to live, there is one group that reversed this pattern.

In 1893, a group of people left Australia to found a colony in Paraguay, South America. They wanted to live in a society that was set up according to their own social ideals. They named the colony New Australia. Some of their descendants are still living there.

Challenges Faced by Migrants

Shopping

When a person cannot understand English well, grocery shopping can be stressful.

Health Care

Working out where to go for a health problem can be difficult when a person is not familiar with their surroundings.

Family

Not having any family nearby can make people feel lonely and isolated.

Lifestyle

Ways of living that are normal in one country may be criticised in others.

Education

Educational qualifications achieved in another country are not always recognised in Australia.

Emergencies

Seeking help in an emergency can be difficult if a person does not speak English well and does not know about the services available.

Legal System

Becoming familiar with Australia's legal system is a challenge to new migrants.

Transport

People need to work out how to use public and private transport without getting lost. This is complicated if a person has difficulty reading signs written in English.

Workers and Skilled Migration

Australia has always needed to import workers. Initially, labour was provided by convicts but, after the late 1860s, they were no longer sent to Australia. The small population of Australia meant that there were not enough workers for farms, shops and industries.

Mass immigration programs were devised to encourage British and other European people to migrate to Australia. Despite these colonial migration schemes, there were still not enough workers. Up until 1901, when the White Australia Policy came into force, people from non-European countries were also allowed to come to Australia to work.

After World War II, another mass migration scheme from Europe provided the workers Australia lacked.

The selection of migrants to Australia today is based on hundreds of work categories for which there are not enough local skilled people to fill the available jobs. These categories change as the economy grows or contracts.

United Kingdom and Ireland

The United Kingdom today includes England, Scotland, Wales and Northern Ireland. Migrants have come from all these areas to start a new life in Australia, and they are collectively called British. London is the capital city of the United Kingdom. The Republic of Ireland became a separate country in 1949 but still forms part of the British Isles.

Since 1788, when the first British colony in Australia was founded, British people have formed the largest group of immigrants. In 2015, there were more people in Australia who had been born in Britain than in any other country.

Between 1860 and 1901, 250,000 people were encouraged to migrate to Queensland from Britain. Because the ships carrying them came from the north, Queensland became the only state to have immigrants settle in a number of small towns along its coast, rather than most going straight to the capital city. Cairns, Townsville and Rockhampton were settled in this way.

There are many reasons why the British influence is so strong in Australia:

- In the 19th century, Britain was a global power, with an empire that covered a quarter of the world's surface. This empire included Australia.
- Australia's parliamentary system has British origins and is based on the Westminster system of government.
- Up until the 1970s, the White Australia Policy restricted the arrival of non-European people.
- Immigration schemes specifically targeted British people, offering them free travel.
- Thousands of British convicts were sent to the Australian colonies. When they had served their sentences many became settlers, seeking to build a British lifestyle in the new colonies.
- The potato famine in the 1800s devastated communities throughout Ireland, leading to massive social and political unrest. Irish people were forced to leave and thousands arrived in Australia, both as settlers and convicts.
- Australia continues to have the British monarch as its Head of State.
- Up until the 1950s, many Australians called Britain the 'mother country'. They sang God Save the Queen as their national anthem, until it was replaced in 1984 by Advance Australia Fair.

	United Kingdom	Australia
Location	Western Europe	South Pacific region (Oceania)
Population	64 million	24 million
Size	242,000 square kilometres	7.6 million square kilometres
Main Languages	English	English

Commonwealth of Nations

The Commonwealth is a group of 52 nations. They meet every two years to discuss issues of common concern. Queen Elizabeth II is Head of the Commonwealth and head of state of 16 Commonwealth countries.

The Commonwealth was formed in 1949 as a group of countries with ties to Britain. This shared history is no longer a basis for membership. The latest two members, Rwanda and Mozambique, do not have a British colonial past.

Scholarships and fellowships are awarded by the United Kingdom to citizens of Commonwealth countries under the Commonwealth Scholarship and Fellowship Plan. The Commonwealth Games for athletes from member countries are held every four years.

War Brides

After World War I, British war brides made the long journey to Australia to marry Australian soldiers they had met in Britain.

Czech Republic and Slovakia

Czechoslovakia was the name of a country in Europe up until 1993. In that year, the country split into the Czech Republic (Czechia) and the Slovak Republic (Slovakia). The capital city of the Czech Republic is Prague and the capital of Slovakia is Bratislava.

During World War II, Czechoslovakia was annexed by Germany. Many Czechoslovakian people sought refuge in other countries. After the war, Australia accepted thousands of Czechoslovakians as refugees.

In 1968, Czechoslovakia was invaded by the Soviet Union. Australia again accepted displaced people as refugees, this time taking about 6,000 Czechoslovakians for resettlement.

	Czech Republic	Slovakia	Australia
Location	Central Europe	Central Europe	South Pacific region (Oceania)
Population	11 million	5 million	24 million
Size	77,000 square kilometres	48,000 square kilometres	7.6 million square kilometres
Main Languages	Czech	Slovak	English

Department of Immigration

Australia's first federal Department of Immigration was created in 1945 to deal with World War II migrants. The majority of these people came from Europe.

Before 1945, each state set its own immigration regulations.

Snowy Mountains Hydro-electric Scheme

The Snowy Mountains Hydro-electric Scheme in New South Wales is one of the most impressive civil engineering projects ever undertaken anywhere worldwide. Sixteen dams, 145 kilometres of tunnels, hundreds of kilometres of piping, a pumping station and nine power stations were constructed between 1949 and 1974 to generate electricity.

Work on the Snowy Scheme began soon after the end of World War II, when Australia had a labour shortage. Thousands of migrants and displaced people escaping the destruction in Europe worked on the Snowy Scheme, which could not have been undertaken without their labour. The workers had to live near the building sites and the accommodation provided for them was basic. Snow and ice during the winters made living conditions harsh.

France

France has a reputation as a cultural and style leader among western nations. The capital city is Paris.

Colonial Era

French naval ships, explorers and scientists visited the Australian colonies on numerous occasions. La Perouse's ship arrived in Botany Bay only a few days after the First Fleet in 1788. Britain and France were at war at various times during Australia's colonial history, and French ships and their crews were welcomed at some times and treated as dangerous enemies at others. The French consulate in Sydney was the first consulate of any nation in the Australian colonies. It operated from the late 1830s.

World Wars

Australians fought in France in both World Wars, forging strong bonds between the two nations.

Migration

Although there have always been relatively few French migrants in Australia, French culture has exerted a strong local influence. French was the leading foreign language taught in Australian schools until recent decades. In the 1950s and 1960s, Australian arts students dreamed of travelling to France and studying at the Sorbonne in Paris—it was equally as desirable a destination as the universities of Cambridge and Oxford in England.

	France	Australia
Location	Western Europe	South Pacific region (Oceania)
Population	67 million	24 million
Size	640,000 square kilometres	7.6 million square kilometres
Main Languages	French	English

Alliance Francaise

The local branch of the Alliance Francaise was founded in Australia in 1895, to spread knowledge about France and the French language.

Marist Brothers

The Marist Brothers' Order was founded by a French priest in 1817. In 1872, the first Australian Marist school began in Sydney, and others followed in quick succession in all the mainland States.

Sorbonne University in Paris

Germany

Germany is a country with an advanced economy and a reputation for engineering excellence. Berlin is the capital city.

Colonial Era

There were two waves of German refugees who arrived in Australia in the colonial era. In the early 1800s, members of the Lutheran church in Germany found it difficult to practise their religion freely. From the 1830s, many German Lutherans migrated to the Australian colonies where they could worship without restrictions. From the mid-1850s, German immigration was actively encouraged to help ease the labour shortages throughout the Australian colonies. The German settlers mostly went to South Australia, where they developed the wine industry, built their Lutheran churches and left German place names as a reminder of their presence.

World Wars

Australia and Germany had tense relations during the 1900s, due to being on opposite sides during both World Wars. During these wars, Germans who had settled in Australia were interned in camps because they were thought to be a security threat. From 1914, hundreds of German prisoners of war and local people of German descent, and even some who were Australian citizens, were interned at the Holsworthy Camp near Sydney.

During World War II, about 7,000 Jewish German people arrived in Australia. They have made a significant contribution to the arts and business in Sydney and Melbourne.

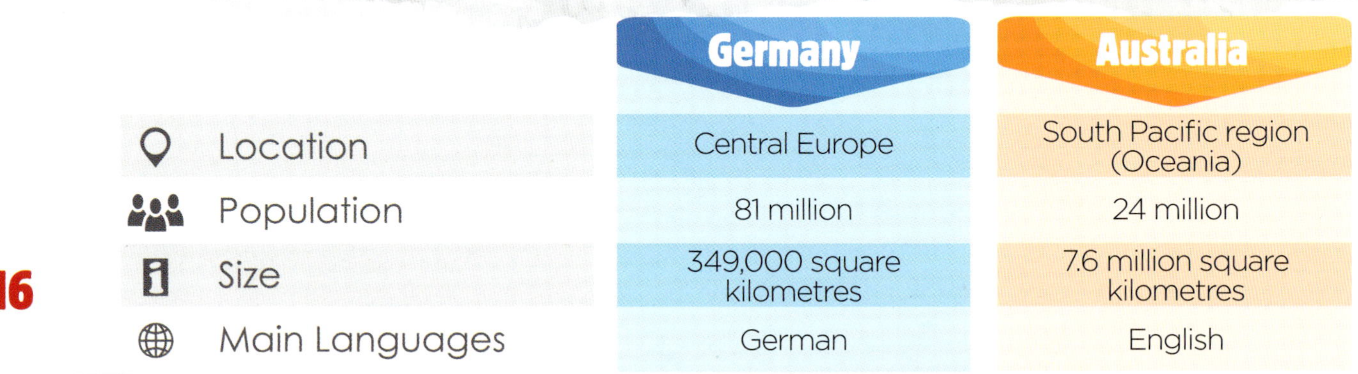

	Germany	Australia
Location	Central Europe	South Pacific region (Oceania)
Population	81 million	24 million
Size	349,000 square kilometres	7.6 million square kilometres
Main Languages	German	English

Dunera Boys

In 1940, 2,500 German men were sent from Britain to Australia on board the Dunera. They were interned as enemies during World War II, even though two thirds of them were Jewish and opposed to the Nazis. The men were sent to the Tatura camp in country New South Wales, but were eventually released. Some of them decided to join the Australian armed forces.

Ludwig Leichhardt

Ludwig Leichhardt, the famous explorer of Australia's north in the 1840s, was from Germany. He disappeared in the desert on his last journey and no trace of him has ever been found.

German Village Shop in Hahndorf, Adelaide Hills area, South Australia

Greece

Greece includes about 400 small islands as well as the mainland. Athens is the capital city. The country's ancient history is also the history of western culture, since the origins of democracy are found in the early system of Greek government, and Greek art and drama have inspired generations of people.

Colonial Era

In 1829, a group of Greek convicts arrived in Sydney. They had been convicted of piracy and had also been fighters in the Greek War of Independence.

The gold rushes of the 1850s attracted Greek miners and settlers. Those who stayed set up businesses and worked in agriculture.

The first Greek Orthodox Church in Australia dates from 1898. Located in Surry Hills in Sydney, Holy Trinity Church became a centre for the Greek community.

1900s

As a result of World War II, thousands of migrants from Greece settled in Australia. After 1952, the Australian government paid for the travel of Greek migrants to attract them to come to Australia and ease the labour shortages experienced after the war. Melbourne has one of the largest Greek communities anywhere outside Greece.

Chain migration was an important pull factor in Greek migration. Greek people already in Australia encouraged family members and others from their home towns in Greece to emigrate. When they arrived in Australia, the new migrants were looked after by family and associations based on towns and regions in Greece. Greek people who have come to Australia include those from the mainland of Greece, as well as people from Cyprus.

The most visible change the Greek migrants made to Australia in the mid-1900s was the establishment of milk bars throughout cities and country towns. Many of these were very attractive places and they offered customers a standard of relaxed but stylish service that had not existed before.

	Greece	Australia
Location	Southern Europe	South Pacific region (Oceania)
Population	11 million	24 million
Size	131,000 square kilometres	7.6 million square kilometres
Main Languages	Greek	English

Lemnos Island Greece

Lemnos

During World War I, the Greek island of Lemnos was the base for thousands of Australian soldiers who fought in the Gallipoli campaign.

Battle of Crete

In 1941 in the Battle of Crete, Australian and Greek soldiers fought together to defend Crete against invasion by Germany.

War damaged ruins in Crete, Greece

Hungary

The capital of Hungary is Budapest.

Some Hungarian people left their country to find a better life after 1849 and after World War I .

After World War II ended in 1945, Hungarians joined the millions of displaced European people seeking refuge in other countries, including Australia.

The Soviet Union moved into Hungary in 1956. Once again, some Hungarian people became refugees. This time they were assisted by the United Nations, which had set up refugee camps from which Australia accepted many Hungarian people.

Despite being relatively small, the Hungarian migrant community has produced a number of people who have risen to prominence in the professions, sports and arts in Australia.

	Hungry	Australia
 Location	Central Europe	South Pacific region (Oceania)
 Population	10 million	24 million
 Size	90,000 square kilometres	7.6 million square kilometres
 Main Languages	Hungarian	English

Members of the Hungarian community marching during Australia Day Parade in Melbourne

1956 Olympic Games in Melbourne

The water polo match between Hungary and the USSR became known as 'Blood in the Water' because of the violence that occurred between the two teams. The Soviets had sent soldiers and tanks into Hungary the month before the Olympics.

During the Olympics, some Hungarian athletes claimed political asylum in Australia.

Frank Lowy

Frank Lowy, founder of the international Westfield Group, was born in Hungary. In 1959, he developed his first shopping centre in Blacktown, near Sydney.

First Synagogue

The first synagogue in Australia was founded in Hobart and was in use from 1845. One of its founders was Hungarian settler, Isaac Friedman.

Italy

Two thousand years ago, the Roman Empire spread from Britain across Europe to Byzantium. The nation of Italy was founded in 1861, following the amalgamation of small states and of Sardinia and Sicily. The capital city is Rome.

Colonial Era

In the 1800s, Italian settlers in Australia included people attracted by the gold rush, others seeking to escape political unrest in Italy, and Italian Roman Catholic priests. The Italian population of the colonies was a mix of professionals, tradesmen, small business people, farmers and labourers. The Italian stonemasons were in high demand for their building skills.

In 1880, a group of Italians were persuaded to pay the Marquis de Rays large amounts of money to settle in an idyllic township in Papua New Guinea. The scheme was a scam and there was no township. When Sir Henry Parkes heard about it in Australia, he sent a ship to collect the Italians and bring them to New South Wales. They arrived in 1881 and eventually formed a settlement called New Italy in northern New South Wales.

1900s

In the 1930s, Italians were prominent in the sugar cane industry in Queensland. In rural New South Wales they settled in Griffith, where their success in agriculture contributed greatly to the reputation of the Murrumbidgee Irrigation Area as a source of produce for the whole state.

World War II

During World War II, many people of Italian ancestry were placed in internment camps. They were released after 1943, when Italy became an ally of Australia in the war against Nazi Germany. After the end of World War II in 1945, large numbers of southern Italians from Calabria and Sicily were among the European refugees and displaced people who travelled to Australia.

Olive Oil

The first Italian migrants to Australia were surprised to find that they could not buy olive oil for cooking. Olive oil was once only sold by chemists in tiny bottles for medicinal use.

	Italy	Australia
Location	Southern Europe	South Pacific region (Oceania)
Population	62 million	24 million
Size	294,000 square kilometres	7.6 million square kilometres
Main Languages	Italian	English

Fast Fact!

In 2015, people born in Italy were the fifth largest group of migrants in Australia.

Little Italy

The Italian community in Sydney's Leichhardt developed a vibrant business district known throughout Sydney as Little Italy.

Eureka Stockade

In 1854, Raffaello Carboni from Italy was the only person to record an eyewitness account of events at the Eureka Stockade.

Anglo-Italian Treaty

In 1883, Italy and Britain signed a treaty which allowed Italians to own property and do business anywhere in the British Empire, including Australia.

Netherlands

The Netherlands is one of the world's leading agricultural exporters. It has a long maritime history, much of it as a global trading power. Rotterdam is the world's largest shipping port. The capital city of the Netherlands is Amsterdam.

Pre-Colonial Era

Dutch ships visited the western and northern coast of Australia from at least the 1600s. Dirk Hartog Island, off Western Australia, is famous for the pewter plate left there in 1616 by Dutch explorer, Dirk Hartog. The plate was engraved with a message and nailed to a piece of wood at Cape Inscription, to inform any future arrivals that the Dutch had been there first. Hartog only found the coast of Australia by mistake, when his ship was blown off course on the way to Indonesia to trade spices.

Colonial Era

A few Dutch people were amongst the convicts sent to the early colonies. Dutch ships sailed between Batavia (now Indonesia) and Australia, supplying the colony with food and goods. Some of the Dutch sailors left their ships and headed for the Victorian goldfields in the 1850s.

World War II

Dutch people living in Indonesia escaped to Australia to avoid the Japanese invasion. Dutch merchant ships formed part of the naval convoys taking equipment and supplies to Australians fighting in the Pacific region.

1950s

In 1951, the Dutch and Australian governments signed a migration agreement which encouraged thousands of Dutch people to settle in Australia. Australia became the destination for 30% of the Dutch emigrants leaving the Netherlands in the 1950s.

	Netherlands	Australia
Location	Western Europe	South Pacific region (Oceania)
Population	17 million	24 million
Size	34,000 square kilometres	7.6 million square kilometres
Main Languages	Dutch	English

The Bonegilla Migrant Camp

In 1947, the Victorian government opened the Bonegilla Centre in Wodonga to house new migrants, most of whom were from Europe. The living conditions were simple and the residents were supposed to find a job as soon as they could.

Being able to speak English gave a person a big advantage. Many different nationalities ended up living near each other in the camp, and there was little privacy.

Bonegilla was closed in 1971. Block 19 is the only building still remaining and it is now a museum.

Poland

Following years of political unrest, Poland is now one of the European Union's most economically successful countries. Its capital is Warsaw.

After the end of World War II, some displaced persons from Poland came to Australia. Among them were Polish soldiers who had fought alongside British troops. Tasmania received over 800 Polish ex-soldiers in the 1940s. These men provided the labour needed to build the state's hydro-electricity schemes.

In the 1980s, more than 25,000 Polish people came to Australia. They were escaping the political unrest in Poland, resulting from the movement for a democratic government and freedom from the USSR.

		Poland	Australia
	Location	Central Europe	South Pacific region (Oceania)
	Population	39 million	24 million
	Size	304,000 square kilometres	7.6 million square kilometres
	Main Languages	Polish	English

Paul Strzelecki

Strzelecki was a Polish geologist and explorer. In 1840, he named Mount Kosciuszko, which is the highest mountain in Australia.

Auschwitz

In 1940, the Nazis established the notorious Auschwitz Concentration Camp in Poland. The Australian Government has assisted in the conservation of this historic site.

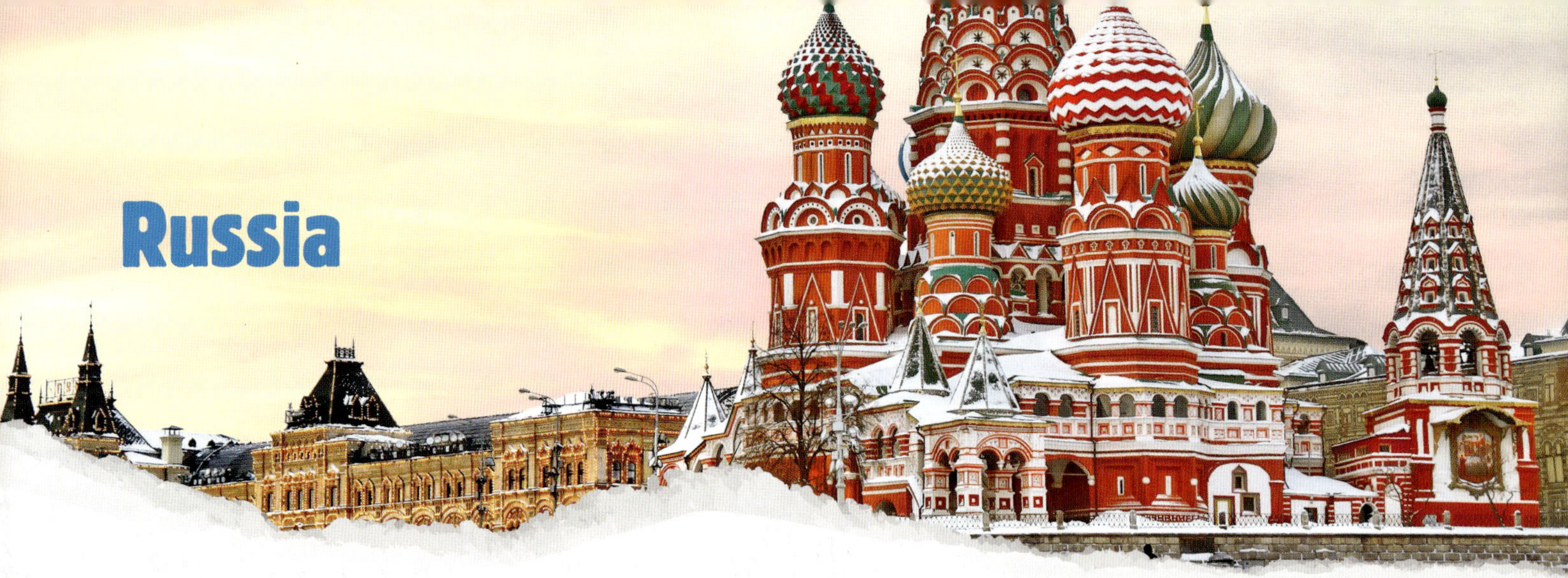

Russia

Russia is the largest country in the world. Its capital city is Moscow.

Colonial Era

Russian ships were frequent visitors to the early colony of New South Wales. The harbour beside the suburb now known as Kirribilli was one of the places where they anchored. Some of the sailors decided to stay in the colony.

At one point in the mid-1850s, Australia began to fear invasion by the Russians. This fear was one of the reasons for positioning cannons on Fort Denison, a tiny island in Sydney Harbour.

After relations settled down, a Russian Consul was appointed in 1857 to look after the interests of Russian migrants in Australia.

1900s

A Russian supporter of the Bolshevik revolution founded the Australian Communist Party in 1920. This revolution resulted in two groups of Russians settling in Australia: the supporters of the communists were called 'red Russians' and those who supported the old Tsarist regime were called 'white Russians'.

St Vladimir's Church was the first Russian Orthodox church in Australia. It was opened in 1942 in Sydney.

Thousands of Russians were among the migrants who arrived after World War II. In return for the Australian government paying their travel costs, the new migrants had to work on government projects for two years.

From the 1950s, Russians who had been living in exile in China were forced to leave, following the rise of the People's Republic of China. More than 7,000 settled in Sydney. One of these migrants, Tania Verstak, became famous throughout Australia when she won the Miss Australia Quest in 1961.

	Russia	Australia
Location	Europe, North Asia	South Pacific region (Oceania)
Population	142 million	24 million
Size	17.1 million square kilometres	7.6 million square kilometres
Main Languages	Russian	English

The Petrov Affair

The Petrov Affair was a high-profile spy scandal which occurred in 1954. Russian diplomat and spy, Vladimir Petrov, asked the Australian government to grant him political asylum, since he feared being killed if he returned to Russia.

Putin Visits Australia

In 2007, President Vladimir Putin became the first Russian head of state to visit Australia.

Ballet

Tickets to performances in Australia by Russian ballet companies, such as the Bolshoi and the Ballets Russes, have been keenly sought by Australians since the 1930s.

Scandinavia

Denmark, Finland, Norway and Sweden

Colonial Era

A number of Scandinavian sailors were on ships that travelled to the Australian colonies.

1850s

The gold rush attracted miners from Scandinavian countries.

1855

Edward Knox, who was born in Denmark, founded the Colonial Sugar Refining Company. CSR sugar is still sold in supermarkets across Australia and 85% of it is exported.

Late 1800s

People in Scandinavia were targeted by the Queensland government in its search for more migrants to fill the local demand for labour. Posters and pamphlets stressed the warm climate and opportunities that migrants would find when they arrived. Migrants were offered assistance in paying for their travel and were promised rural land grants. On arrival, some of the Scandinavians found the hot, dry climate unbearable and moved further south.

World War II

Norwegian ships and their crew contributed to the naval convoys which supplied the Australian wartime operations in the South Pacific and Indian Ocean regions.

1957

Danish architect, Jørn Utzon, won a competition to design the Sydney Opera House.

Yugoslavia

The kingdom of Yugoslavia was formed in 1929. It became a communist republic in 1945, encompassing Croatia, Serbia (including Kosovo), Macedonia, Montenegro, Slovenia plus Bosnia and Herzegovina.

After World War II

Yugoslavian people arrived in Australia as part of the mass migration schemes after World War II. Over 100,000 people from Yugoslavia arrived in Australia from the 1960s onwards.

Balkan Wars

The Balkan Wars in the 1990s resulted in a further 30,000 Slavs arriving in Australia, as part of Australia's humanitarian program. In 1993, the United Nations established the International Criminal Tribunal for the Former Yugoslavia. The role of this tribunal is to deal with war crimes and crimes against humanity.

The countries which once formed Yugoslavia have made strides in overcoming the economic upheaval of the Balkan Wars. Croatia is now a popular tourist destination for visitors from around the world, and the historic coastal city of Dubrovnik attracts many Australian tourists.

Visit these websites to find out more about migration to Australia from Europe:

www.migrationheritage.nsw.gov.au

www.emelbourne.net.au

www.sbs.com.au/immigrationnation

Glossary

annex	add a region to a country
consul	person who looks after people from their own country in a foreign land
convoy	group of ships
enshrine	protect
infrastructure	organisations, buildings and equipment needed for a large project
property title	confirmation of ownership of a property
revolution	overthrow of a government
Tsar	Emperor of Russia
war brides	women who married or became engaged to Australian members of the armed forces overseas during wartime

---

Index